bl(A)nk

Mark Cunningham

bl(A)nk
©2023 by Mark Cunningham
All rights reserved.
Published by Mark Cunningham
ISBN 979-8-9882957-1-6

Thanks to Linda Kobert, Christopher Simmons, harry k stammer, Amy Stephenson, and Mark Young.

Cover photograph by Makoto Tsuka on Unsplash.

Section 3 appeared in *Otoliths*.

Parts of Section 4 were used in *multizon(e)*, a collaborative project with text by Mark Cunningham and video by Dale Wisely, which appeared in *Right Hand Pointing*. <www.issues.righthandpointing.net/multizone>.

bl(A)nk

1.
[gathere]

stray
st(all)

erratcetera
errat*a*

a/miss
spewn

flos(s)

no/w

a-crystall

intensift
e-vent

b/lures:
no is
to noise

surf/d

                                                  unclosed
                                                  pre-veil

                     mar(ge)

thr(um)b

circlull
nubble

                                                  secreted
                                                  sill
                                                  still secret
                                                  oopsaline

anat

                      crisis
                      in(ter)vent
                      ion

lurt
spazzle
bubbles

                      quarter
                      bent
                      foraminin
                      ferral
                      semi-
                      conditions

microheric
accler
rashunt
similar to
disappear

        crimpush

pourly
developed
seep
wavy
thickinings
1/possible
more
-scene
than
-seen

O void
or ovoid
could be
mis(p)rent

concres
sense
narrows
line of
concrea
sense
almost co-
insides

marginall
similar to
absent

vulved
alonglong
axes

                              finely itted
                              surface
                              usually
                              present
                              almost
                              angulariat

hape con
widevate
fluctuen
trawl
pararind
ordocar
vivuate

                              very
                              almost

radiate
semi-rad
data
monoporc
ellopaquriz
ed
softable

        test dark in
        in(c/s)cide
        n'tlight

tremenos
drom(n)ia

semi-
stat(ic)
s*alien*ity
underinse
meander
clot
percystent
kinettle

tremore/le
ssh

    ho(i)st
    he(a)ve

                                               mite

                    priviledge

  in
  contenant

                              comepass
                            threshold

              passed
              tense

                              un*if*ereniat

~~sheare~~

              emit
              time

pha(i)sm
v(ort)ex

outriff(t)   a/rest

a/rest   outtiff(t)

spectrim
specktrun

f/ray   collu/ide

verglike
floata(i)me
ossillation

  pell

                                                abyssail

                                                valladome
                                                semi-co
                                                a-certid
                                                covery

                                                inturnity
                                                internity

                        salvage
                        selvage
                        sealvague

                        phost
                        boss spate

crustal pap
set up par

z/one

                                  res orbs
                                  s(t)eep

                                  numburr

cl/inch

                                  (f)un(d)us

                                  n/or
                                  lurch

                                                            tropause
                                                           (o)pen
                                                           c(lot)ter
                                                           winn(d)ow

                                                ploswivel
                                                blocage

                        a-ranged
                        longit
                        unserial
                        mum
                        vina orbig

conrest
concreep

                                                con-
                                                secrete-
                                                tion/shun

insula(r)
infusarea
impload
indetour

incessed
tent
namalouse
a lotment
strata a-
gem

occur(d)

goad/goed
engine

nasend
hold

primordial
premodeal

inner
opp   runnell
poseable   lull
            recoil
transmutt   re:run

sp(h)ar(a)
mat

mercurry

            mini-
            chooser
more   limbo
honer   brace
menu

imcroprob
al
elliptick

erupt
(c)rate

                                            tract sally
                                            try start
                                            sty tar
                                            tar lace

                        vividivied
                        crevace

                        granulose
                        merge
                        vent
                        mid
                        ealevol
no in-   surfface
dillable   midian
node of(f)   to gra(s)ph
point of(f)

                                            bestirubble
                                            valease

                        motile litter
                        hive
                        volt thrum
roll curl
code dice
meld cull

                                            usable rive
                                            bale/bail
                                            virusettle
                                            vivetube

                                                        e(a)cho
                                                        cohere
                                                        castarry
                                                        retractrawl
statrace

                        leaser cue
                        tap(s)pool

                                                        accre(a)
                                                        sense
circuimage

                        cyclocks

                                                        magnifi
                                                        scufficent
ante-tear
antero
pointed   chemo
narrowidge   crush
                                                        loner enroll

                        hon/me
                        base

~~ou~~nce

18

nerobic
brocade
cab
index
(s)orb
nib bin
caroma
index
not brace

       de(e)mo
       t(e)em   me(e)ted
                        pellet
                        pleat
                        mo(a)ttle
                        dea(l)lt
                        mote

anged
dangles
snared
dreg   leach grip
drag   calliperill
                                      other

gel denser
edge
gnarl den
lenses

                                    glitch itch
                                    legit
                                    reap

                        ventual
                        lineafocal
                        l(i/e)int
                                                misfitem
                                                caddyin
                                                decidice's
                                                decideddy
                                                vim eve
real reel
ani-brine
arc rein roil
line coil
rail(l)
calibrace
caliburr
calipar
bear *off*
bare on
                        slime lime
                        pile
                        simpill
                        pull
                        primlim(b)
                        sample rip
                        preamble
                        bleep blip
                        c(r)ease
                        spill
glober
plan(k)
gameto
genecyst
crust
delopes

		celapane(l)
		missteep
	rapid	d/rift code
	recurs	riff code
	staid	
		tepid
		sssipat
	careous	
	can(all/ull)	
	gellate	
	rineboid	
		micromeet
	thropoc	
	onsept	orbisema
	saclul	bassail
		rundt
	spiroiled	
	lab	fract
	develoop	fact(r)rail
	as	
	slit	
		tide/tide
addvent		arcituck
		-taxy

gear lint
tangle
(t)angle
thr(all)
halt(er)
g(r)ain

ba[sic]

tinge
rein

waterwelte
rayaw

not
negated
adderant   lull
wateear   line
bar   intrance
careen
container   spurrupt
reach   blur(t) tube
de/canter

spate
skate   hanging
litter
adopt   elan(e)
adept
adapt

grit
patchit
till(t)

molt/en
acord(i)on
atavis(i)ita
dis/spell

mono
c(l)ue

node
bet(ter)

ultra-
viole-
levitilt-

reel
reseep
tic(k)le
percal
clamp
t/race
demelt

tad poll
dot delta
datum

stypt bellm

                          limig
plect

idem
mid-yep

pert scrap
peps tide

s/platter
rasp
leap
acut(t)er
reappeel
spate lure
pasture
sack
staples
bec(l)auss
set-up
treacleat
placer
capsule
purl
a.s.a.p.
sputa atlas

per use
per ruse

primed
demo
trim tempo
rel(a)y ploy

                                                                 quixessent
                                                                 stra
                                                                 ngement
                                                                 eclectricity
                        sheltear   destill
                                                                  diff/
                                                                 deferaction

fullg(u)rant

                        floadtation

retie
retrier
retire

                                                                  f(l)ail

                                                                  elid
                                                                  meddly
                                                                  ramp port
coarse   lim/ned
intense
or missing

cargket

                        bail

                        ba(i)llet

                                                last

                                                glyserum

        bas(t)ed

        mutative
        thermal
        hoverote
        at all

pro-carry

inunfolding
overundon
fuious
mean(en)-
durring

subo(a)rd
junct
s/lag

e(l)idol*on*

tarry
are/era

one(rouse)

2. *[eAT]*

                                                                   dis/tention

retain
peel

                                                                    sort
                                                                   sort of
                                                                   detained

semi-mise

                                                                   com(op)osite
                                                                   spand

fa(u)lter t(r)oll
lowcater

                                                                   prop(s)zipper

sociate

                                                                   penitrabble
                                                                   premismear
                                                                   nutation
                                                                   errea

invesrend
inversand

load
lode

                                                                   ~~diffe ring~~
                                                                   homegering

cumminae
ration

                              verging
                              sillts
                              -ated
dissodial   boundary

                              temp(o)-prise
ranged

                              c(raw)
string(n/m)esst

                              grouped
tingearnetide   a-spersion

anti-dote

                              inf(l)at
                              motiff
preen
ring
re-wrung
                              instigate
                              gist
                              sort
scour
arc

radiarent
motil motent
cav(e)ate

gelid glide

bit
b(it)e

pseudo-
byfurcat'em

perseive

subbsidemall

snare
relay

rills
or
ills

kaleid

spurrung

prune
nudge

mid edge
midge
ledge

                                        opposing
                                        areposing
                                        re-posing
                                        apo(i)sing

stemm(h)er(e)

                                        gear
                                        grip

loci
sally

modified
-tic
-tag
iso-topic

                                        st(et)utter

hem
mend
dilate
details

                                        from
                                        form
                                        cornucop

                                        at/t(r)end

ratiions

                                        impacted
                                        snoop
                                        compendia

moot
mort
tone

                                        sp*end*?

emp/tied

                                        tapped
                                        tad

particle
article
particu(r/l)ating

                                        hmm
                                        mend

sag
bar

                                          interseep
                                          flyer/filer/
                                          piler/pliar

deformode

                                          at tack
                                          phrge
                                          min(e)im

form
from

                                          re-bus re bus

hereby
here by
redone

                                          universerial
crop

                                          no dos aria
                                          ergence omen
                                          probeably

this
harried

                                        nucleoconstru
                                        crunch

urg
surge
series

                                        sn(ick)
                                        s(lick)

phased
dearth

                                        boss
                                        rigor

a null
amburr
twowayer
ceeding

                                        passt

(h)ur(d)ge

                                        juvennile

                                        whorl
                                        increase

incorpsosreal

quor

popct

marcate

culact

pourt

gnawt

vi(an)de

de(s)pot

lapse(e)d

resona*ting*est

incramment

discr*eate*

hereor(e)

aggr/lutinate

s(h)ift

tretch

transfor

usu(r)pper

calciosilensea

attachk

fewed

a-send

codaced

re(z/s)onate

                        rapid
                        (in)stall
anamosey

nibblurr

                        uncoiled
ingulf   sidevex
                        de-finite
                        w/range

(s)ur-round

hysteriospheri
call

                        reful
init_o_id   refuel
micro heric   refulgence
for(m)
for um

                        one weigh

spry
delay
unit

strained
dittos

mostly semi-
notype

re-rail
st(r)ayed
snare

modelide
lid
g(l)ides
diss

snarl
(tr)end

thresh hold

incomepass

ryne
scaloris

abhaste
tummel

                              f(l)atten

portinteve(e)rs
unequell
psedu-bullimia
innergin
agonitic
real lumina

                              ferm-
                              ent(h)avtive

trap zoidal
poly-gones
no gerd
trichoke

                              gestour

w/rung

                              unfilltered
                              diverseive
                              was/te
                              teme*no*s

open
danger
p(a/u)rse
pen
ping

reloadcate
some
lo(o)se

upgraide
propourtion

mesoincriprint
abysstince

omphalost

hashforminferi
or
gra/dual
puncturation
equilibrim

more -un
later rally
prescid
less latered

sedisament

missspent

                                        ~~pause~~

ensure
endure
ensues

                                        formstruck
                                        formsuck
                                        formstruct

not(h)ing
edit

                                        out hitch
                                        outsticher

de/comp
de/camp

                                        spagitall collar
                                        grye-ration

ingulfant
tadpeal

                                        insuccretion

pubbled
win*now*

ediable

delitterious
jetsum

planoburr
best flat rally
annullerate cal
careous
mmetrickle

trifle filter
groops
net fit

verglic
jetsame

                                             intra/inter
                                               pour
                                               poor
                                               pore

clump
surffield
surffeeled

                                             feedbu/ack
                                             uncoiled
                                             sidevex
                                             wr/anglupe

de-finite
noose
spree

                                             sutuational

add
mine/us

3. *[f(l)ight]*

—or—overlaps
rid nos
sutu
situ

at tack

scrab

mire simmer melee
ram(a)ble amber

it(ch)

ti*died*

coalesion
coalesson

over throes

smeary brevity

veto
trove

vergegis(t)ave

several lets

penestrata

gassed
vertigo

got
deviates

ri/vet

alter
topo
(t)rope

overove

rev(e)ile

proton
tromp
pronto

ranted
gore

skigrapple

atraction

trans-however axis
errupted entiferent

pordcellanawall
translitt(er)ed
coribperture

(end)ure

de(s)tirred

insert
runtier
inturn

raverse

vag(ue)inull aggland

ex-ta(i)nt
ecstant

fractroll
fractoll

inciden-

raxis

pentriat

mutegenetic
hadron
musttard

logphragmo(i)de
rusevelope

lesson(e)

irrpairable

fenddent

ubble

irrataculation
rizontal tical
rows *out*
zoncressocket
ariable lateline

exagonal

arid vap(a)id rut
visieve site

stai~~nd~~

pla(nk)tonic
sp(here)idal

sthit

differrent

re(a)made

droved

counter-clockwise
stepid
equa(i)nt
sinsitrial

specull formaging
liposcene

interupt

messh

asymmetry
shimmy

vary ing
iferous(t)
bluntspin
onertwo
lower permi-
numb-er one

fined
fus(s)ed
rally

tyro shiver

veryvex sum
randed
ends

jurid(r)iffferespondera

thin-alled

pres(s)urd
f(ort)

(p)repare

overa(r)m
stymy

bluntip
either only
or bull

junk = sail
junk = sink
sometimes even

be-have
retry

insiderinse

(w)rapt

partiall

-unching
-alles(s)

arbitraitor

orb it
hive
or bit
thrive

amb(l)er
rev

abor/absortive

-(t)r(i)ent

litters

render

err
de/scend

rea(l)m

reprograin
vim/mer

variabiliviensis
discrux

en(d)gage

per burr
dial link canals

scle(a)rosion

corustraytion

f/loss

a/bout

~~co~~here

agonago(o)n a/go

transmundaim
nomad(e)
invicta(l)

pre-macrodation
incigestion

gro(u)per

lariate

avert
vaster
avast

blot
par

therm rover
vibrat ory
be-rate
servo

tot(st)al(l)

~~sur~~cease

surdcease

test orb void
cont(in)ue spyral

a-gain

ramshackle
repeat

blip
lip
bartear
re-(p)ort

celed

incorpeel

phyizzel

apart
a-part
a part

filament
moshun
coll(o)idialstick
parabbled

transtressive

predamentor

de-ranged
re(t)read

beta
potter

dissg(org)e

di-

4. *[nexTus]*

                        bore-   dare
                        board-

drift action
    raction

                                         (w)hole

diffuser

                                       sphool

differentrial

                                       fillaments

different(i)
able

                                       somtim/nes

difluefence

                                     memb/ran

difficu(l)t

                                   even(t)strew

diffusat
diffract

                                   s(pl)it
                                   sp(i)l(l)/it

                              modif
                              modrif
                              modifeed

           -vide)

    cataepistro   claustrophy
    p(h)ic(k)

                    phraising

sp(r)iculite
singalongate

        subterm
        transmargin
        tag

                      inside vim:
                      there.
        no lateral   abductor
        chambers.   tusscles
        no pillar.   in vertical.
        past tense   simple pour
        of *steal on*   canal
        still on?   diffeo-
                      (o)lded
                      phism.
                      a periodic
                      aperidoic
lo(o)se   phases
siphone   escap(e)ace
rhizocrust

o
r
i
caulpend
a
l it/out

                      along

                      f(l)attened
                      outline,
                      unserial

stub born

der-
lock-
star-
ette-
polynanno
rills

poly-gone
pyramiss

telescropic

                                              lengt
                                        -ellerella-
                                                         i
                                            span

acute(e)
perforitphery
involens
apertive   conclus*if*t
unseptarate:
areal, not a
real

interrim

celiap(l)ane

　　　　　　　　line (ne)ear
　　　　　　　　t(r)ic
　　　　　　　　　i
　　　　　　　　　c
　　　　　　　　portal

hangle
laceae
onsist

　　　　　　　　　　　　　　　　riftersial
　　　　　　　　　　　　　　　　　eftersial
f(r)acture　　　　　　　　　　　　f
　　　　　　　them/ore　　　　terseal
　　　　　　　themerrier

actrual　　　　prenumbera

　　　　　　　　　　　　　　fus(e)
　　　　　　　　　　　　　　cuspade:
　　　　　　　　　　　　　　deal try/tri
　　　　　　　　　　　　　　re:symn:
　　　　　　　　　　　　　　res(e)(i)nd
winnowhop
ping

smeggle

                                        mers not so
                                        pronounced.
                                        a marginal
inconmmins   (f)rill
foarmemes
richoshed,
irratum
chro(a)mes

interconnec
ting co(a)sts

                    po(u)res
                    very
                    fine.
                    oop-haped.
                    loop-shaped.
                    a pert cess,
                    reevous.
                    site: vex side

                                        mar/gin.
                                        s(tr)uction.
                                        bath zone.
                                        culate
                                        septulope.
                                        irregate

assembslag
assemblsag

                                    memberis
                                    d(a/e)nce
                                    appearand =
                                    appariand.
interrim   a/typical

nowtation

rhinen

                    n/somadolog
                    stasisquall

                                    focusp inoc
                                    lashstick
                                    sticks
lag   fumehood
tributearoff   inagerius
d(is)placed.
vage.
often rally

                    maximini
                    assemblast

                    interst

                              each end
                              bifurcated.
                              does not
       ratiraptour   conneck
       allrays   at corners.
       equal *n*th   a rant
                                  spun(ge)

                              testoiled-
                              turbintum-
                              annammina-
                              pyrapile
                              half-who
                              genarent

                                                          f(r)oamy
                                                          cruddle

                              previous:
                            pervious.
                            now si(e)vi-
                            perk

multi-win
      n
    paradil
   ari
     v
      e   noninaffini
       d   ties
                                                           tessembling

for(k)ing
im/age(k)ick

                                                    dullary shell

                     reflic(r)ater
                     surf(r)ace
                     ossillation
                     (d)rifter

morp haus
copdid(e)a
remo(a)te

irrugla/op

fore curve
void
recurvoid

                    elongout
                    r(o)uts.
                    minor necks
                    ax
                    verygate

                    laps/lashoid
                        p
                        u
                    melaliran

                                        percystomes
                                        persisthome

bipola(i)r
    nter
      conec
corral   choruscation
    late
      xten
      ded   lasp(h)inge

                                surc(r)ease
scle(a)row

            tire? free.
            (p)resent.
            exstir(n)ally sp(l)end or
            a sm(all)   gleeand
            de(press)ion

                                assess
                                  o
                                  ry
                                a(pert)
in(e)vasions   u
                                present,
                                vari
                                able

            neo-pan
*can*descent   ridge.
            marginall
            unshorened.
            allmost
            completely
            lost

                        condont

                                       exits
                                         x
                      young -in   i
                      later -on   s
                      radipert   t

apert(o)ure
in visible   frondicul
                      aria

                                         b(l)inds.
tubelon   siteli(n)es
w   o
o   n
     g
shorter third
in-compete

                                       resolotion
                                       re(slot)ion

                    aborbridginal

long whirled
thin/thick
juven(v)ari
um

                                        b(r)im
                                        completent.
                                        -de(a)d in
                                        two lob(e)s

                        post-seep
                        continected

no(u)npro
midi-*um*
fruffg(r)ab

                                        door: stall
                                        view.
                                        somewhat
                                        wavy.
                                        locall
                                        situated

multiun(i)for
med

                        l
                        trans
                         y
                         e
                         r
paraquater

nit(r)oglyd
scence

ssitude

                                        phaedarian
                                        palynomorph

atmanyatam

                                                  very all

            half-moon
            antunna
            neither
            high-tied nor
            low-tied.
            smooth
            sockets

sub-pry form

                                    left valve
                                    overlaps
                                    right
                                    right valve
                                    overlaps left
                                    left valve
                                    overlaps
                                    right
                                    right?

                vert ort.
                  r
                phic

quadrate,
subsea/t,
hom(e)broial
longitudineel
sometimes
distinct
si(c)ted.
others -lique
cription:
(b)road
(z)one
numera/edial

hingingine

                                        delu(r)g
                                        explosure

                 g
                 o
                 t
              holes
                   h
                got
                 l
-like   e
s

                                      transitional
                                        stages
                                        only,
                                        re-markable
                                        occu-rinse

micoherico-
cu(e)rinse

                              pert forplete

                    pestilents
                    pestilense

local omen
rift.
filamentrill.
loci raft

                    f(r)ill
                    marginail
                    but forward
                    swing
                    extremiable

                                        ur-assic
                                        spinitial
                                        part straight

                    prop a gate
                    muunple
                    rimple
                    ingradient

a long
e(c)llispe

                                            rest/art

                                            org/b

usu-ally right
istribution

                    ellipticle.
                    sometimes
                    has a
                    central
                    process
                                            two cycles
                                            of elements
                                            generally
                                            on the *is*tall
                                            s(l)ide
                    inf(l)ect
                    limnoil
                    molten
                    (c)leave
                    molt f(l)it
                    molten
                    cleft

inact inter
loot tool:
formatt
co-late
(m)all.
film flim.
trial trail:
(f/l)oam
t/race

                          asterisk

                                            sixteen
                                            predico
                                          me(n)ts

                                          s
                                         e
                                           c
                                             o
                                      rigginallly
                                             d

ch/amber

        gartaintral
        demnstrata
        burs(st)
        laps(e)

                            epileaptiform

passive dip:
visited.
diva tip
pries:
aced.
edit parse.

                          imperfcreted
                          echoles

                          involv/involut
                          in-ary
                          umbilgeneus
                          stallized stru

            similaminate
            rideation

r
e
apare/pair

protozone
borealesses
fus(s/e) line

segwait

neoflabell
amphiscaler
amphiscatter

onslic(e)

folds not
i/enforced

ondice(e)

a-
-a

tremendumb
tremenrun
tremendone:
one side =
last whirl
displayced:
rectagland:
ornabet
weenation:
moreplext
t(o)ures
for(m):
sut(s)ures
mis(s)ing/
uncalcicon
nex(t)ulous

                    side few
                    very/vary
                    void, cross-
                    section
                    rarely,
                    initiall
                    ellipse
                    sometimes.
                    has lopped
                    several
                    times
                    independ
                    endtlyl:
                    relatively
                    (f)olded
                    without
                    centrawl
                    funnelpoly
                    seamus:

                                                       half
                                                       (in)closing
                                                       externill
                                                       light
                                                       inner dark.
                                                       longitugnal
                                                       sweeps.
                                                       senter not
                                                       center

                          hemicall
                          astring

or-
namoment-
(r)ation =
g(r)ainu   an cesstir
lation.
grate
grap(h)ic
importsance

                          hemicall
                          astring

                                                 s
                                                 nettle
                                                 i
                                                 c
                                                 k

                          repeti(l)tion

                          polyseemus

cast

                                        (n)arrow
                                        he(a)vron-
                                        shaped
                                        narswider
                                        iterative

incounter

                  redeagang
                  dereranged
                  range

peroadiate
prolocus
recystivative

                                        prolocus
                                        flexstyle
                                        polylectic
                                        microw
                                        cornuscope

megafuse-
spheric
side tunnels
only

                                        frag/gell
refurigor

remi-septive
pole to pole

rhizone

                                                          spareagmos

              abraceons

secondary
transviral
usiform
neo-
wag(g)er

                                          p
                                          a
                                          r
                                   (f)usalina
                                          u
                                          s
                                          s

                                    mani(c/fe)
                                    sessation

                    sting of
                    tech-
                    and thec-

                                    almost
                                    completely
pseudo-wag: absent
eventuall   two-thirds
evenly/lea   of length
folded

three layers
of narrow
oles

                    p
                    r
                    o
                    por/centralis

                young form
                micromargin
                null:
                later stages
                sparse
                same rate
                persal.
                lank
                inframension
                place t(w)o
                place

direcliquely
ward.   fourked
stiped
namanation   revingenes
and a further

                entelucky

                                          min/uses
                                          c(rink)
                                          conknots
                                          amass

                torn a do
                applifecation

corddors   corridooors

monlamellar
utradiate
tax per pend

                -rude
                -stems

ortho-gone
rangundular
ultracarbo
nat(al/ed)
perforrate

                                  co
                                  ax
                                  all

                                  egree

                                logaridgmic
                                stations
                                lickp(l)an

                spiwhorl
                moseyaic.
                accree(p)tio
                surfacoiling
                atedge
twomorrow

                                    fraglasm
                                    (st/ra)tion

                    p
                    pres
                        sed

spin:
consuctive
horizons
insingle
layer
(insing)
(insinge)

                                    sp(r)iral.
                                    rally podia.
                                    agglate
                                    apetture

                    erruginous
                    inrustations

                                    chiastozy
                                    (gr/p)ace

                    test uloc

                    fussijous

sometimes
replaced
with pseudo-
sequal

                    fus(s)elag:
                    sub
                    equidimens
                    on
                    miclog.
                    geneous:
                    addvance
                    int(w)o

lozoncalatio
bi-
strata(fet)ish
clay
coscreep

                                    ampi-*x*

        scenaruno

                    learm

        lentcullin

        spiral
        volutedice
        rig dor: alt.
        bet ween.
        ire vent

                                    laiyrd
                                    sprazzle

tesxtual
rina:
gglut

                                                                  total
                                                                  versity

                                                                  bar(r)ed by
                                                                  ridge.
                                                                  ___varrier

umbilis*qua*
morline(e)
skellato
(s)cene

adventill
felxostile
miliolining

                                  undertmined
                                  detour/mine
                                  determound

                                        s-shaped or
                                        oval
                                        or circuliar:
                                        related
                                        to one *and*:/
                                        ollow
                                        cessetude
                                        (g)lobul
                                        areollow
                                        solidrods
                                        disscentrica
                                        tally:/
                                        modiloose
                                        mesh.
                                        test void
                                        void test:/

                    (s/l)ea(k/d):/

sharp edge
veryvex:/
v-curve
fluctuates
often forms
continuous
ridge,
ventral arts
pro-node:/
more or less.
often both:/
equivalve
ace:/
quadriloll:/
cannopil(e):/
-lacytheme:/

rounded
n/ails
below
margin:
ornatia
laterface.
central one
closed

                                        re-rent
                                        or namented
                                        with pap

weak-
me(a)nted
valves
with median
sulc.
extremely-
rated velum
forms velum
(p)ouch

                                        numerous
                                        distinct pits.
                                        contract.
                                        ovi-cribbed

                              r(oo/oa)m
                                                  microclog
                                                  ranulayer
                                                  not incruded

                              cording
                              core ding

long sents

                                                  pubblead
init-used
f/sutures.
each =
other.
or knot
                                                  fossillabe

                                                  demislid
                                                  inte(a)rlater
                                                  clearoblast

                              overla/op
                              *if*fers

exexexist
                                                  rotic delta

                              ample rares
                              meta-laced

Also by Mark Cunningham

morfact. Independently published. (2023).

sort/quantum. Independently published. (2023).

A Longer Life. Text with video by Dale Wisely. (2022). YouTube. <https://youtu.be/cSWPjndC7fM>.

Future Words. if p then q. (2020).

"f(l)ights." *Otoliths* 56 (Southern Summer 2020). A 110-piece sequence. <www.the-otolith.blogspot.com/2020/01/mark-cunningham.html>.

"Fail Lure." *Otoliths* 52 (Southern Summer 2019). An 81-piece sequence. <www.the-otolith.blogspot.com/2018/11/mark-cunningham.html>.

multizon(e). Text with video by Dale Wisely. Right Hand Pointing. (2019). <www.issues.righthandpointing.net/multizone>.

Alphabetical Basho. (2016). <www.beardofbees.com/pubs/Alphabetical_Basho.pdf>.

And Suddenly It's Evening. Beard of Bees. (2014). <www.beardofbees.com/pubs/And_Suddenly_Its_Evening.pdf>.

Regularly Scheduled. Beard of Bees. (2012). <www.beardofbees.com/pubs/Regularly_Scheduled.pdf>.

Scissors and Starfish. Right Hand Pointing. (2012).

Helicotremors. Otoliths. (2012).

specimens. BlazeVOX. (2011).

nightlightnight. With photographs by Mel Nichols. Right Hand Pointing. (2009). <www.archives.righthandpointing/com/nightlightnight>.

71 Leaves. BlazeVOX. (2008). <www.blazevox.org/ebk-mCunningham%20REAL.pdf>.

80 Beetles. Otoliths. (2008).

Body Language. Tarpaulin Sky Press. (2008).

www.ingramcontent.com/pod-product-compliance
Lightning Source LLC
Chambersburg PA
CBHW051708040426
42446CB00008B/786

Gift from God

What you are about to read is a true story about a yellow and black swallowtail butterfly and me. On September 6, 2002, my mother and I had gone shopping in Cameron Village, which has outside shops, and we were walking along approaching Jolly's Jewelers when a yellow and black swallowtail butterfly landed on my left breast. I did not see it coming towards me and needless to say I couldn't believe my eyes and what I was seeing. This butterfly was beautiful and was not trying to free herself from my top. She was content and I said, to my mom, "What am I going to do? I can't go in a store with a butterfly attached to me." My mother was in awe, as was I. I put my finger out to see if she would step up on it and she did. The butterfly didn't fly away and remained on my finger. I lifted her up several times in the air to see if she wanted to fly away, but the butterfly still stayed with me.

I knew I was experiencing a spiritual revelation from God and when you are open to all God has for you blessings come in all kinds of ways. I decided to sit down on a bench still holding the butterfly high above my head and then she flew off and out of sight.

These were the words that came to me; "***I will give you the desires of your heart***". The color yellow means Gift from God.

On August 31, 2003, almost a year later, I was at home and it had been raining, a thunderstorm had just passed and I went out back of my townhouse through my sliding glass doors and looked down and saw a beautiful yellow and black swallowtail butterfly lying flat to my patio. She was still intact, no marks or tears in her wings or body. The butterfly had no bugs on her and I tried to pry her loose but she was stuck to my patio.

On all my outside doors, I have an angel armor shield sticker with Psalms 91:11 "for He will command his angels concerning you to guard you in all your ways". It was like the butterfly had been placed between my two sliding glass doors – protection, safe until I could rescue her.

I realized that this is the end of my story almost one year later her final destiny to be close to me. God always gives me wonderful blessings and this beautiful butterfly came home to die and give me hope and encouragement for my future.

God loves all his creations and my prayer is that my butterfly story will be passed on through you. Now when you see a yellow and black swallowtail butterfly, I hope you will remember my story and why this butterfly is so special to me – God's gift to me, now my gift to you.

I. SPIRITUAL DREAMS

What Are Spiritual Dreams?

Spiritual Dreams are a Gift from God. After I accepted Jesus Christ into my heart and started on my spiritual journey with Him, then the Spiritual Dreams were activated in my life.

Spiritual Dreams are different from other dreams because of how God communicates with the Holy Spirit within me. When God talks to me through a Spiritual Dream it is like revealing a part of a puzzle. I ask the Holy Spirit to help me understand the interpretation and He does.

There is purpose in each Spiritual Dream the Lord has given me. The true indication of a Spiritual Dream is that it is God-centered and to be awakened immediately so you can remember every detail.

For many years, I have written my Spiritual Dreams in journals and as I am typing the Holy Spirit is revealing the interpretations.

God connects with me as he reveals what I need to know through my Spiritual Dreams. This is the desire of my heart to hear from God.

Each Spiritual Dream has encouraged and matured my spiritual walk with the Lord.

Seeing Jesus

My dream began at a church meeting where a woman was talking. Since there were no chairs left up front I was sitting on the floor.

The woman started to lead us in prayer and I had my head bowed and my eyes closed. When the prayer was over I raised my head and opened my eyes.

The focus in the room was a picture on the wall. It was a large glass rectangular picture frame. A lady in the audience said, I see Jesus and I looked and Jesus came into clear view.

Jesus appeared with an angel behind him and was wearing a white robe. His hair was long like many photographs I have seen of him.

Jesus revealed himself in the picture frame to give encouragement and hope to the ones who desired to see Him.

Jesus was smiling at me revealed that He is pleased with me.

Gifts and Surprises

In my dream, I found an 8-1/2 x 11 office manila envelope. On the outside of this envelope was a pair of sunglasses. One of the arms on the sunglasses was broken.

When I looked deeper inside the envelope there were three surprises, a matching pair of beautiful golden topaz earrings and ring set in 14k gold surrounded by smaller blue stones.

The golden color of the Topaz stone and the surrounding blue stones represent Spiritual Gifts from God that he is using in my life to help others in need.

In previous jobs, there have been promises broken as in the sunglasses on the outside of this envelope. The Lord intends to restore what was lost and broken to a place of beauty and financial freedom in Him.

The Lord gave me encouragement and hope through this dream that He has many gifts and surprises waiting for me.

In His Arms

My brother and I were walking along in my dream. There were tall buildings and steps going up and I felt lost but my brother was there. I was carrying him in my arms for a while and then he was carrying me in his arms.

I told my brother this must be what it feels like to have Jesus carry you. I felt safe, secure, peaceful and totally relaxed and unafraid.

The Lord revealed to me that my brother and I trust each other and the Lord with our lives. The tall buildings represent fear about where our lives are going but the steps going up represents hope and encouragement that we are desiring to move up into the things of God.

When we both felt lost, we carried each other, but Jesus revealed to me that He wants to carry us through any problems that we may have.

Connected to God

As my dream began, I was in a room with two women and one of the women started to sing and worship God and immediately she started to levitate in a vertical position straight up to the ceiling.

After she finished singing the song she was lowered back to the floor. I asked her, "does this happen every time you sing to the Lord"? She said, yes. I was amazed.

I also remember while the lady was singing in mid-air, I felt the spirit of the Lord very strong around me.

The Lord revealed to me that three women being together were symbolic. Three meaning Father, Son, and Holy Spirit.

My desire is to be open and experience all God has for me.

Favor with God

    On September 3, 2002, my brother, sister-in-law and I were walking towards a large white ship that was docked. The focus of my dream was my brother talking with the captain. My sister-in-law and I were standing together on the dock away from my brother and the captain. She was dressed in a nautical white and gold short outfit and looked very nice. I left my brother and sister-in-law at the ship and walked away alone.

    The Lord revealed that the large ship represented a huge blessing from God for my brother and sister-in-law. The ship being solid white is a spiritual blessing and my brother's favor with the captain is also favor with God. My sister-in-law's white and gold outfit is symbolic of God's spiritual blessings coming their way soon.

    In my dream, my sister-in-law was not pregnant which indicated that God's blessing would come after she delivered my nephew on September 11, 2002.

    On October 25, 2002, my Spiritual dream came true and my brother and sister-in-law received a large sum of money enough to pay off their home. God's blessing to them and a healthy baby boy, too!

    When I walked away from the ship this indicated I will also receive a huge blessing from God but my blessing will come later.

Surrounded by God's Love

There was a group of people boarding a ship when my dream began. I would have to hurry to catch up with them and it would be late when the ship returned. I was uncertain about going on this ship. As I was heading out of the building, an older woman came up to me and said, do not go with that group on the ship.

I immediately saw coins on the ground and started to pick them up when I noticed a very unique coin, smaller than a penny, and flat with a symbol of a bird. This coin did not have a date.

There were lambs surrounding me. As I was petting them I could feel their wool in my hands and then I awoke.

This woman was saying to me to stand firm right where I am. Trust in God as indicated by all the coins I picked up on the ground that He will not only provide everything I need but guide my steps along the way.

This unique bird coin represents the Holy Spirit and the power He has in my life. God brought his lambs to surround me with His peace and comfort me with His love.

Determined to Survive

In my dream, there were three people in a car. Two were in the front seat and one in the back. I was sitting on the passenger side of the car.

We were heading down a cliff for a long time and I thought it was the end of my life. When we came to a stop the car was hanging off the rocks.

I was determined not to give up so I opened the right door and to my amazement, I was at the top of the cliff and walked out on land.

The Lord revealed this car represented my life. I was sitting on the passenger's side of the car (not in the driver's seat) indicating that the Lord is in control of my life.

Even though the situation seemed hopeless, I never gave up hope that the Lord would rescue me as indicated by me opening the door and being at the top of the cliff and walking out on land.

Jesus Loves Me

My mother and I were in this dream walking down a hallway towards an office. When I looked out the office window I saw in the distance a hospital surrounded by water. There were cars driving through the water but it was not deep. As I looked out the window, I was at peace and happy. We decided to leave this room and the door shut behind us. I immediately turned around and knew I didn't shut the door. We started walking back down the hallway when two men approached us grabbed our arms pulling us back into the office. I was trying to pray out loud but my words were coming out soft and quiet.

These evil men thought we were there to obtain information about them. They had to kill us and I was given a drug by mouth. This is how I responded to their evil actions towards me; I started singing, "Jesus Loves Me." I awoke from this dream and realized I was alive.

What comes out of a person's mouth is in their heart. I have never been prouder than what came out of my mouth, "Jesus Loves Me" and He really does.

Call on Jesus

A large brown snake was approaching my front door. In my dream, I was trying to open my door and get inside but the snake was moving closer so I closed the door and moved away. I was talking to the Lord in my thoughts and the Lord immediately soared me straight up into the sky.

But when I got into the sky, there was a large black object right in front of me and I said, JESUS out loud and it exploded in a million pieces right in front of my eyes. When I looked below the snake was quickly moving away from my front door.

The Holy Spirit revealed to me that my door represented entrance, not only entrance into my home but entrance into my Spirit. The snake represented a demonic attack and by me choosing to move away, the devil would not have an opening to enter. The Lord has shown me many times that I can communicate with Him through my thoughts and He will hear and rescue me. When I got up into the sky I thought I was away from danger but then there was another black object to confront. Black in a dream represents evil but I knew by saying the Name of Jesus out loud, demons would flee and in this case explode! This was a Warning Dream to be careful that the devil is looking for an entrance but the Lord is always watching over and protecting me from any danger.

Sensing Danger

In my dream, I was talking with a lady in her 80's. In front of her face I saw a large spider web with black spiders and told her not to move.

The black spider web represented evil and by me removing it set her free from the devil that was trying to control her mind.

I have been praying for her salvation and the Lord was letting me see she was in danger.

The Lord gave me this dream to warn her that the devil was trying to steal her salvation.

It would be a shame to get to the end of your life and realize you missed eternity with Jesus Christ.

God never gives up on anyone so I pray she took my Dream seriously!

God's Protection

I was working in a stressful job and given promises that were never delivered.

The Lord gave me a dream that I was wading in a shallow stream of water where snakes had been. I only saw their skins and rattles in the water. I knew from this dream God was warning me about the people I was working with.

Snakes represent warning, deception, and danger. The snake skins were my co-workers' attitude towards me – they disliked me (Christ inside of me). The rattles floating in the water were the harsh words, threats, and critical spirits being directed at me. The shallow water was about their dishonesty over promises made to me.

God is always watching over and protecting me from harm. I knew the Lord was giving me this Dream to stay alert to the dangers all around me and to continue to pray and seek the Lord's direction.

Even though I was going through rough waters, I felt God's peace all around and through me.

Center of God's Will

As my Spiritual Dream began, I was in a restaurant and the focus was a round table with only a tablecloth. There were no chairs or people sitting at this table.

Underneath the table I saw a Kennedy half-dollar and picked it up. Kennedy was facing the front of the coin instead of his profile.

There were dimes surrounding the Kennedy half-dollar. Every time I would pick up a dime, I saw another one to retrieve. My hands and pockets were full of coins.

A round table represents Spiritual such as grace, mercy, compassion and forgiveness. The tablecloth is God's protection over my life.

Kennedy facing the front of the half-dollar represents heart.

The Kennedy half-dollar and dimes were found in the center underneath the table. Being in the center of God's Will is the best place to be.

Dimes (10) represent times of trials and testing but the Kennedy half-dollar (50) means my service is acceptable to God.

He will use every trial and test I go through to reflect His glory in my life.

Hanging onto Jesus

I was standing at the top of the stairs looking down to the first floor when my dream began. I could see two women working in the kitchen that was adjacent to the living room. The focus was a large wall hanging that hung over the railing. I do not know how it happened but I lost my balance and started to fall over the railing. I remember trying to grab hold of the wall hanging but I was falling too fast. Then all of a sudden the Lord stepped in and everything started happening in slow motion, my fall slowed down and when I landed on the 1st floor, my body was still shaking. Before hitting the floor, I felt a hand on the left side of my face protecting me from the fall. When I opened my eyes, I was fine, no broken bones or bruises.

The Lord gave me nine words to share with these women "the left side of your body is the Lord's". I remember one of the ladies said that she saw me fall but did not rush over to me. They both stayed at a distance but were concerned about me.

The Holy Spirit revealed to me that upstairs is a spiritual prayer place and face represents my heart. When I was falling, I tried to grab hold of the wall hanging but I knew only God could save me from this fall. God's hand protected the left side of my face as well as my body. God slowed down my fall to show me that nothing is impossible with Him when we believe.

I did not understand why I had this dream but I knew the Holy Spirit would reveal it to me in time.

The same night I had this dream, my mother had a horrible fall at a Christian Couples Retreat in South Carolina. My mother was walking up some stairs and lost her balance and fell forward hitting her face on a beam. Her nose was broken and she had numerous stitches.

When my parents checked into their room earlier, my mother found a dime underneath a table and picked it up saying, here are my 10 blessings from God. My mother told me later there were 10 people to help her when she fell (as indicated by the dime she found earlier in her room).

My mother decided not to call me until she returned home to North Carolina. The Lord revealed my mother's fall to me through a Spiritual Dream to prepare my heart that He would take good care of her and she would be fine. My mother has healed completely and I thank God for his protection.

Looking for Heavenly Blessings

I was standing on a white floor when my dream began. I saw two shiny pennies; one face up and one face down. They were within a couple of inches from each other. I picked the pennies up and was excited about finding them! As I was walking around, I came back to the same area and there were more coins. I was excited about finding so many pennies!

I decided to come back the third time and found two special coins on the floor. These coins were gold and had detailed carvings on both sides. One coin was an Angel directly facing the front of the coin in full armor; even the helmet was detailed in design. It was not meant for me to know what the second coin looked like, but I knew that these gold coins were not from this earth but from Heaven. I remember putting these coins in my pocket so I could examine every detail through my magnifying glass but I never got the chance before I awoke.

Money represents spiritual gifts in a dream and how the Lord intends to use my life to help encourage others in their walk with God. When the penny was face up, I was looking up to God for His blessings and when the penny was face down, God was looking down to bless me.

The Lord gave me two special gold coins to say I have heavenly blessings waiting for you; trust me with your life and you will receive more blessings than you can ever hold in your hands.

Flying Above Danger

It was nighttime and the focus of my dream was a white straight back chair with no arms or cushions. This chair was unique and perfect because it could fly above the trees.

At first I thought I would fall out but I held on to the seat with my hands.

When I felt danger, I would immediately jump in the chair and the chair would take me up into the sky.

The Lord revealed that the chair represented Him. My dependency and trust is in the Lord completely.

I did not say any words out loud only in my thoughts and the Lord would rescue me.

To Believe

    I was in a room of people and the focus of my dream was a woman sitting across from me. She looked at me and said, I would like to levitate and I closed my eyes to pray but I started going up instead of her.

    I straightened out vertical because I had been in a sitting position. When I was near the ceiling of this room, I called out to the people below look up, I'm in the air.

    Some people looked up but most of the people didn't even notice or see me. The Lord revealed to me that this woman did not go up because her lack of faith to believe she could. She was relying and depending upon my faith to help her rise to the ceiling.

    God rewarded me because of my faith and trust is in Him completely. The people who saw me in the air believed and the ones who didn't were spiritually blind to the things of God.

Surrender All

In my dream, I was walking alone and heading down a dirt road that was unfinished and noticed to my right a huge body of water. It had started to over flow down the embankment and in the path where I was walking. I was startled by how fast the water was flowing so I started to head back where I came from but couldn't because the water was flowing on all sides of me.

The water was so tall and wide; I knew the only way out was through. As I tried to push myself through the water, I knew I couldn't do it alone.

I surrendered my hands and arms straight up to the heavens and Jesus rescued me just in time to see the waters below flooding in the path where I had been walking. Jesus lifted me up in the sky; high above the water that was in my path.

The Lord revealed that the water represented fear about where my job was heading but my trust is in Him.

Jesus took me out of danger when I surrendered all to Him.

Ministering to Women

I was walking in my dream toward a small village store to meet Diane. When I went inside the store Diane was not there but an older lady with short blonde hair in a bun. She took my hand and we flew upward and then we were in a different place – streets were narrow and this woman asked me if I had ever ridden a bike? I said, yes then two bikes were brought up to be our transportation.

When I looked down at my feet, I had on flip-flops and knew I had the wrong type of shoes to ride a bicycle. As I started to get on the bike – my dream changed and I was in a small room in Memphis, Tennessee talking with 5 or 6 blonde haired women in their mid 20's.

One lady seemed to be an angel and I had questions to ask her but as I was sitting on the floor talking to these women all of a sudden my body became vertical and I went up to the ceiling with my palms up – it was like I felt no gravity.

I felt the Holy Spirit all through me – chills from the top of my head to the souls of my feet – even my hands tingled. It was a wonderful feeling. I remember saying, as I sat on the floor, here I go again – floating upward.

The Lord revealed that this older woman was an angel sent to help me on my mission. The narrow road represents a new life.

The bike represented the work God has called me to do for Him but I felt unprepared as indicated by the flip-flops I was wearing.

When the dream changed, I was in Tennessee talking to 5 or 6 women. I knew this was God's mission that I minister to women. Their blonde hair symbolized that this mission is a Gift from God being prepared for me.

When I started to rise to the ceiling with my palms facing upward, I was asking the Holy Spirit to anoint my hands to accomplish what the Lord is calling me to do for Him.

Soaring in the Spirit

The Lord gave me my first Soaring Dream. Soaring Dreams are different from Flying Dreams because of the depth that I am in the Spirit. I am so connected to the Lord as I am traveling through the sky at an incredible fast speed.

When I am flying or soaring in a dream, the Lord communicates with me through His thoughts and I do the same with Him. We are in tune with each other so completely that words do not need to be spoken out loud. It is so incredible and exciting!

When I awake, I feel rested like I have been on vacation for a week. It is the most wonderful peaceful feeling in the world.

In this dream, I was soaring through the sky at a very fast speed and did not know what was up ahead but I was not afraid because the Lord was with me.

When I came down to the ground it had been snowing and I asked someone how much had it snowed and they told me 6 inches. When I left it was warm and sunny. I stepped down deep into the snow and then I awoke.

The Lord revealed to me even though I could not see what was up ahead of me that my trust is in Him completely and He was guiding my way.

Snow represents New Beginnings and when I stepped down deep in the snow, the desire of my heart is to experience the deeper things of God and connect more with the Holy Spirit

Levitate in the Spirit

I was awakened around 3 a.m. by a dog barking in the distance. As I lay awake for 1-1/2 hours the Lord put me back to sleep and gave me an incredible Spiritual Dream!

I was in a large white house upstairs praying in my office. As I was sitting on the floor I started to straighten out vertical and rise to the ceiling. I could feel the ceiling on the palms of my hands. As my dream continued, I left the house to find my mother and share with her what the Lord revealed to me.

The Lord is going to let me levitate in the Spirit. He also told me that most people only receive this gift when they go to Heaven but the Lord was going to let me experience this in my waking moments. How exciting is this and precious of the Lord to give me such an incredible gift!

In Spiritual Dreams, a house represents me. By the house being large and white is my desire to know more about God. As I was praying I felt connected to God and the Holy Spirit and am excited what the Lord is teaching me through each Spiritual Dream.

Power of the Holy Spirit

I was with a friend in a very old brick building when darkness surrounded us. In my dream, I saw something moving across the floor but could not see what it was. It appeared to be the size of a cat. In that moment, the Lord soared me up to the ceiling, which was very high up and away from danger. When I got to the ceiling, I floated from one light to the other and could feel its heat. When it was safe I returned to the floor. I remember it was the most wonderful feeling being in the Spirit.

I went next door where a prayer meeting had just concluded and as I was entering a woman came up to me and placed her hands over my ears. She knew I had been in the presence of the Lord and said some prophetic words over me. Since my friend had seen me rise, I asked her to tell the others what she saw.

Darkness in a dream represents danger as in a demonic attack so when I awoke, I immediately started to pray for God's protection over my family. When I soared to the ceiling, the Lord was taking me out of danger to keep me close to Him until it was safe to return below.

Floating from one light to the other is my desire to be connected to the Lord's power, which is the Holy Spirit.

When I entered the prayer meeting next door and the woman placed her hands over my ears and spoke prophetic words, she was bestowing the blessings of hearing and understanding the things of God. I am grateful to the Lord that He is allowing me to see more signs and wonders in the Spirit as I continue to grow in my relationship with Him.

Heavenly Home

    I was standing alone in a very large white building in my dream. There were all open areas and I walked up to my own private balcony and looked out. This white building was very high up with large open windows. It was very beautiful and peaceful.

    As I was looking out, I heard voices and saw people standing in their own open balconies. In the middle of this open area, I saw a room where people were coming together, so I joined them. I did not know anyone nor did I carry on a conversation. Then I awoke.

    This Spiritual place was my heavenly home with my own private balcony. It looked like a home found in ancient Greece. There was no furniture as indicated that I didn't live there yet but this home was being prepared for me.

    White in a Spiritual Dream is pure and this building represented my heavenly home. I had my own private balcony so I could have private time with God but also there was an open room so I could enjoy fellowship with other Christians.

    Heaven is a place of perfect peace.

In the Future

In March 2002, I had the most awesome dream! I was in a big church. There was a pulpit behind the larger sanctuary where a black preacher in a robe was speaking. I was the only person sitting and the preacher called me up to pray for me. As I was walking to him, I never reached him because I started falling backwards.

As I started to fall no one was behind to catch me but I was not afraid. It was like being gently lowered to the floor. When I was on the floor I didn't hear anything only silenced. I said, I'm listening God.

When I was walking toward the speaker before I went under the Spirit the preacher turned into a putty matter, a block of brown like a brick and landed on the floor like a thump. I know this sounds strange but this is what happened.

While I was lying on the floor waiting on God to talk to me – several people from the congregation continually walked around me in a circle and my mom and dad were in that group. When I got up I had a microphone in my hand – like I had been singing or talking.

I started walking back to the front of the church and Marilyn Hickey (minister) was walking towards me.

In the second part of this dream, there were several rooms behind this main room where I had gone under the Spirit. I was with three women and we were standing in the center of this room where you could see several rooms in different directions. Most of the walls were green and one of the women told me that God had painted these walls but they were not completed.

In one of the small hallways there was a wall painted half green and half yellow and I placed my hands on this wall. I felt such electricity go through my body but I was not afraid. I felt peaceful and was in awe of God's work.

As I was standing in this small hallway, I saw a larger room at the back. It had a gold and green tapestry painted on the entire wall – it was the most beautiful picture of a city. It was finished but I didn't see this up close only at a distance.

This church represented congregation and the black preacher was symbolic because God had put him in charge as a leader. When this preacher turning into a brick, it showed me that God is going to take some preachers out of the pulpit that should not be there.

The circle of people walking around me is God's protection over my life. When I saw Marilyn Hickey in my dream, I knew she is a woman of faith and that my life would also be a blessing in the lives of women.

In the second part my dream were 3 women – 3 represents the Father, Son and Holy Spirit. We were all standing in the center of the Main Room – symbolic that I am in the center of God's Will. By the painted walls not being finished – God isn't finished with me, yet.

My desire was to touch this wall so I could experience the Holy Spirit flowing through me and to be more connected to God. Gold (Glory of God) and Green (God's love) are symbolic that the New Jerusalem is completed.

Seeing the New Jerusalem in the distance meant in the future.

Name of Jesus

When my dream began, I was in a building walking behind a man from India and we were heading through a glass window foyer. As we got outside, this man hit the white brick walkway, struggling to get up but couldn't. He was having trouble breathing. It was like his body was glued to this white brick walkway and his body started to melt.

His eyes were following me as I walked around him in a circle saying, Jesus, Jesus, Jesus. Then a miracle happened, his body started coming back to life again. I said restore and this man's body were restored through the Name of Jesus.

The Lord revealed to me that this man from India was spiritually lost and the glass foyer that we both passed through was God's grace. As we headed outside this building he dropped under the power of God (as indicated by the white brick walkway).

His body started to melt and was heading straight to hell but by me saying the Name of Jesus, his life was spared.

Jesus says, choose me and you will have Eternal Life.

II. RELEASING YOUR FAITH

Forgive and Release

How do you handle hurtful comments? Do you lash back? Pout? Cry? Run away? Some people put up a wall to protect their hearts from getting hurt again.

This is one tactic of the devil to use the people closest to you so you will be caught off guard to hurt you.

We all go through hurts but how we respond is key.

Ask the Holy Spirit to show you people in your life that have hurt you verbally, emotionally or physically. Then pray and ask the Lord to help you forgive and release them to Him and replace those hurts with His love.

This is what Jesus did when He was hanging on the Cross. "Father, forgive them for they know not what they do". Say this over each person that has hurt you.

You will receive incredible joy and peace as you forgive and release them to the Lord.

<u>Relinquish Your Problems</u>

It is sometimes hard to let go when I have been praying so long for God to answer my prayers. It is human nature to want to help God out when our prayers are not being answered as quickly as we think they should. This is when we can get into trouble by stepping ahead of God and getting out of His Will.

When you pray believing and trusting God, He hears your prayers and is working something more wonderful out for you than you could possibly make happen on your own.

God has shown me that if I relinquish my problems to Him that He will open the door to the answers I need in my life.

I open my Bible, place my problems inside and relinquish them to the Lord and close my Bible. This action releases me from worry about problems I have no control over.

Relinquishing all my problems is key in God giving me His peace.

Trusting Through Tests

Many prayers I have prayed have been answered in a timely manner, while other prayers have taken a long time. There is always a reason for the delay. Even though I cannot see what is going on behind the scenes, the Lord is working this out for my good. My part is to trust Him.

Sometimes this is a test by God to see how I will respond to a given problem. When the test is over and my response is favorable to God, then I will receive my blessing. If I do not pass the test, I will most likely have to go through the test again.

At the end of my life when I am standing before God, He is not going to ask me how much money I made or what kind of job title I had. He is going to ask me, how did you trust me through it all?

My prayer is I have passed all the tests He put before me.

Trusting God is the key to living my life to its fullest.

Restoring Right Relationships

Easter Sunday I went to the most incredible service I have ever attended! As I walked into the church, I saw a bridge that extended across the entire front of the church. The preacher shared about building right relationships with Jesus Christ and each other. He also talked about broken relationships that needed repair and healing.

In recent years, I have had difficulty communicating with my dad and brother and knew this was the day for restoration! As the preacher concluded his message, he asked if we would take a step and walk across the bridge as a commitment to God to restore those broken relationships. I walked across the bridge and made a commitment to God that day, I would talk to my dad and brother.

I telephoned my brother when I returned home from church and we talked on the phone and I apologized for anything I had said or done that would hurt our relationship with each other. It was probably the hardest thing I have ever had to do but I did it with God's help and he forgave me.

Then I drove to my parent's home and after dinner, I had a real heart to heart with my dad and told him, I appreciate you, I love you and please forgive me if I have hurt you in anyway. My dad listened as I shared from my heart and he forgave me. Easter Sunday was a healing day for me. God's timing is always perfect timing and I thank God He forgave me.

Sometimes it may not always be your fault why a relationship is not working as it should but I can say, there is healing when you ask for forgiveness. I had the most peaceful night's sleep.

III. TRUSTING GOD

Being Thankful

True happiness comes out of a grateful heart to God. When I look around and see the Blessings of God over my life – I thank God! Time is so precious and I want God to use my life for His purpose and plan. Eternity is forever and forever and there are two places where you will live when you die – Heaven or Hell.

When you have a thankful heart, grumbling and complaining go right out the window - pray that you will stay far away from these destructive emotions – remember the Israelites, they wandered around the desert for 40 years and died. They never got a chance to enter into the Promise Land.

The desire of my heart is that you will invite Jesus Christ into your heart and live your life for Him and when you take your last breath on this earth you will be with Jesus Christ forever.

The key to living a fruitful life is to be thankful for what you have. This is what brings true joy and happiness!

In His Hands

Who is controlling your life? If you answered, I am. Maybe up to now, you have been getting along fine without God and surviving.

The reason you have been getting along fine is one person or many people have been praying for you. It is God's protection over your life that has kept you secure and safe.

God examines each heart and looks for someone who places complete trust in His hands. Giving up control is not giving up but relying on a God who has your very best interest at heart.

Maybe you say, I cannot give up control of my life and I do not want to. God will not work in your life without your permission.

As you pray and open your heart to the Lord, He will reveal any area that is keeping you from knowing God's will for your life.

Key to receiving all God has for me will come from placing control in His hands.

Praising God

Many people have gone through storms that took everything they had. How do you Praise God when you have lost everything?

Do you look at your life and say, well, I have nothing or do you say, I am still alive and for this I am Praising God.

You really find out what you are made of when you go through a terrible disaster. It can break your Spirit or make you stronger.

How can I Praise God when all I want to do is cry? Pour out your heart to God – He is listening! Maybe you have never been on your knees before God – maybe it is time you did.

Prayer to God

I do not understand why this happened to me but God I am going to Praise You through this disaster. I want to trust you with my life because I know you will never leave me nor forsake me. Please help me rebuild my life and give me hope and a future. I need you God. Thank you for listening and answering my prayer. Amen.

Broken Key

    I was driving home to my apartment one Friday night around 11:00 p.m. and there was a chill in the night air and I was ready to get inside for the night. During the past week, I had been having difficulty with my apartment door lock, so I would put my key inside the lock and use my foot to push it in and then I could unlock my door. The key wouldn't go in as before and I used more pressure with my foot. This time my key went in too far and broke off in the lock.

    My first reaction was panic, what am I going to do? It is 11:00 at night and all my doors and windows are locked and there is no way to get in my apartment. I remembered a grocer store was open 24 hours and I drove there and called my brother. When I got my brother on the phone, he told me to call the management company and they would have someone on call to help me – so I waited in my car praying until the man arrived.

    Finally this man came and went upstairs to my apartment and looked at my door lock. He tried many things inside the lock but could not get my broken key out. It was stuck inside the lock. As he was trying, I had walked down to the bottom stairs and continued to pray. As I was praying the Lord revealed to me to take my ¼ broken key that was in my hand and put it inside the lock and God would make it whole.

I went upstairs and the man who had stopped working on my lock said to me, "I am going to have to call a locksmith on Monday because I can't fix your door lock." I told him, I know this might sound strange but I am going to put this broken key inside the lock and I need your strength to turn the doorknob and the door will open.

At first, he looked at me with disbelief but did what I asked and the door opened. I was so excited knowing what God had just done and this man and I will never forget that we experienced a Miracle from God.

Since then I have bought a new townhouse and I proudly display my broken key reminding me that God gave me a Miracle that night when He answered my prayers and I am so thankful He did.

IV. HEART TO HEART

Heart for God

Having a heart for God is being open to everything God has for you. God wants you to totally trust him even though you may not understand or see what is up ahead.

A heart that is hungry for the things of God wants to praise and worship him, read the Bible, be around other believers, and cherish the time you spend with God growing in your faith.

What comes out of a person's mouth is in their heart – good or bad. God knows the heart of each person.

Keeping your heart healthy starts with forgiveness. If you are holding any unforgiveness or sin in your heart, your heart is not pure before God. By asking the Lord daily to cleanse your heart keeps you in tune with him.

This makes God happy – a heart that longs to be with Him!

<u>Preparing Your Heart</u>

I start my morning by praising and thanking the Lord for the day. All throughout the day, I am talking and sharing my heart with the Lord.

I first ask the Lord to forgive me for any sin in my life (conscious or unconscious) and if I am holding any unforgiveness in my heart towards anyone to forgive me. If this is hard, ask the Lord to help you forgive anyone who has wronged you.

This is very important: your heart, soul and spirit needs to be clean before your prayers will be heard from God.

Each day, I put on the Full Armor of God like my clothes. Ephesians 6: 11-17 states, I put on the Helmet of Salvation, the Sword of the Spirit, the Breastplate of Righteousness, the Girdle of Truth and the Sandals of Peace going forth proclaiming the Name of the Lord Jesus Christ. The Full Armor of God is God's protection over his children against the evilness of this world.

After I put on the Full Armor of God, I plead the Blood of Jesus over my back, my mind, my thoughts, my body, my soul, my spirit, my heart, my eyes, my ears, what comes out of my mouth and every opening in my body I pray for God's protection.

Pleading the Blood of Jesus is one of the most powerful prayers of protection you can pray.

I plead the Blood of Jesus over any negative emotions that would cause me pain or anyone else and that would be Anger, Frustration, Loneliness, Self-Pity, Doubt, Fear, Impatience, Jealousy, Lack of Confidence, Being Over Sensitive, Being Offended, Emotional Spending, Over Eating, Stress, Anxiety, Worry, Guilt and Shame.

I plead the Blood of Jesus over my house and have this scripture on each door Psalms 91:11 "for He commands His angels to guard you in all your ways".

I plead the Blood of Jesus over my car for God's protection anywhere I might drive or park my car and say Psalms 94:7 "Angels encamp around those who love the Lord".

I pray for God's protection over my dreams as I sleep and God's peace to be inside and around me.

Daily Prayers keep me connected to God, Jesus and the Holy Spirit. I pray that if the Lord can use my life to help someone in need, I am available. I am always amazed how many times the Lord has connected me with someone already praying and I show up and the Lord gives me His words of encouragement to help them.

Being available and sensitive to the Holy Spirit is key in God using my life.

Loving Heart

God is love. God loved me first before I was ever born. When God sent his Son, Jesus Christ into this world, he was saying – I love you.

Before I came to Christ, there was a hole in my heart that I tried to fill with the things of this world and was never completely happy. Only through the love of Christ my heart is made whole.

Jesus brought me joy for my mourning, happiness for my sorrow, peace for my emptiness and a love like I have never known.

The Lord's love is so contagious and exciting that the desire of my heart is to share his love with others.

The key is to pray and connect to the Lord. His love flows through my life into the hearts of people that are searching and reaching out to Him.

Center of My Heart

People that are self-centered want their prayers answered, now!

Who is in the center of your heart? Happiness comes out of putting God in the center of our hearts. God is the only one who can bring true love, joy, and peace in our hearts when we are centered on Him.

Start thanking God for your blessings. I list them one by one. Try it. When you count your blessings you are putting your thoughts on God instead of yourself.

Get involved in a friend's life. This takes the focus off of your life and puts it on someone else.

There is a calming effect that flows over you when you are reading God's Word.

This will keep your heart centered on God.

My Whole Heart

As I was writing this book I sense in my spirit that I was separating myself from my family and friends. It was at this time that the Lord and I became so connected that my writings took on a deeper and higher level.

I longed to share my heart about what the Lord was teaching me though this book but wanted to stay focused on what He was calling me to do for Him.

The Lord showed me that He wanted me to love Him with my whole heart. I always thought I had this kind of love with the Lord but realized he was not first in my heart. My mother and I have always had this love with each other.

There were times I wondered if anyone had ever felt a love like this. It was then that I experienced God's love in a fresh and new way.

God brought me closer to Him that I may know just how much He loves me!

As I keep God first in my heart this love overflows to others.

V. PRAYERS

Making Time for God

We all receive the same amount of time in a given day but how we choose to spend our time reflects what is most important to us.

How much time do you spend with your husband, wife, and children? Most of us would say, not enough. To enjoy spending time with your family is making time to want to be with them. This truly makes each family member know that they are loved, appreciated and valued.

God also wants us to make time for Him. He loved you before you were born. God created you to have a relationship with Him. When you choose time with God this says He is important to you. You are giving God what He desires most, your love, praise and honor.

Maybe you like to sing, play a musical instrument, or dance before the Lord. However you choose, spending time with God not only enriches your life but in the many lives you touch.

God wants to reveal himself to you. He is waiting for you to choose to spend time with Him.

Pray About Everything

Prayer is the most important key in keeping Close to God. When I need anything, I pray. When I am having a problem, I pray. When everything is fine, I pray.

God desires to give me His biggest blessing. All He asks is that I believe and trust Him. I may not receive everything my heart desires but I will receive a better blessing because my Father in Heaven knows exactly what I need before I even ask.

When you pray, be specific for what you want. You will be amazed that your prayer will be answered far and beyond what you asked for.

Start thanking God for your blessing. God delights in His children being excited when they receive a Blessing from Him!

I had been praying for a good pair of sunglasses that would protect my eyes and be reasonably priced.

Having received a new store membership card I decided to stop by and try on some sunglasses. I immediately spotted a pair of Gucci Sunglasses and they fit my face perfectly but only needed a tiny adjustment.

This store did not have an Optical Center so I went to another store. As the lady was adjusting my glasses she asked me for the item number so she could order a pair for herself. As she looked on the computer for the item number, there was no number listed for my Gucci Sunglasses. I knew God had selected these sunglasses just for me!

Gucci Sunglasses usually retail around $200 to $300 since they are made in Italy. All the sunglasses I tried on before were more expensive and didn't fit my face. I thought these were probably too expensive, but when I asked the saleslady she said, they were under $30.00 including tax.

When I prayed the Lord answered my prayers far and beyond what I asked for.

Thank you Lord for my Gucci Sunglasses, great quality, an incredible price and wonderful protection for my eyes!

Fast and Pray

Many Christians fast and pray. Fasting is going without food or drink to seek God in an answer to a prayer or repentance. Jesus fasted 40 days and 40 nights.

The Lord has awakened me many times during the night to pray. Sometimes I would pray for several hours and sometimes a short time. I ask the Lord if there is someone who needs prayer. Sometimes a name comes to me and I pray for that person. After I pray I ask the Lord to put me back to sleep and He does. Sometimes He gives me a Spiritual Dream!

The time between the Lord and me is very special because He has my undivided attention. This is another type of fasting – giving up sleep to pray and seek the Lord.

You would think I would feel sluggish and tired the next day but just to the contrary, I feel energized and excited about my day!

When the Lord awakens me in the morning hours, He is saying, I miss you. I want to talk to you. Spend time with me!

Firework Prayers

Prayers that reach Heaven's door are prayers that are prayed from a person who has their complete faith and trust in Jesus Christ and not only share their faith but lives it.

I have a very dear friend that once told me when a prayer is prayed with complete faith and trust in Jesus Christ that their prayers go up to Heaven like fireworks – exploding in Heaven! These prayers are heard by God and answered.

When a person prays with little faith, their prayers go up to Heaven like a little poof and then they evaporate.

The only prayer God hears from a sinner's heart is the Prayer of Repentance.

We all need prayer from others to help encourage our walk with the Lord. Be careful if you are totally relying on someone else to pray for you. The Lord wants you to pray and trust Him for the answers you need in your life.

Living a life of faith and trust in Jesus Christ is key in God answering your prayers.

VI. GOD'S BLESSINGS

Gift of Love

What brings me true happiness is giving out of my heart to someone who is not expecting it. I love to see their face light up and smile when I give them special gifts just as the Lord does with me.

Several years ago, the Lord gave me an idea of starting a birthday tradition with my friends. I give them a special piece of jewelry that I own. The desire of my heart is to see my friends enjoy wearing my jewelry instead of passing these blessings along after I am gone.

As I pray the Lord always helps me select the ideal piece of jewelry for each friend. This makes their birthday surprise even more special.

I am always amazed how they will respond to receiving this gift. I'm sure the Lord is delighted when He sees me excited with the gifts He gives to me.

The key to being truly happy is to allow the Lord to use your life in the lives of others. The Lord has blessed me far and above anything I have ever wanted or needed.

I Am Home

This is one of my biggest blessings from the Lord. After praying for many years for a home of my own, the Lord answered my prayers and I bought my first new townhouse in March of 2001. I looked at two townhouses in the same subdivision but they were sold. I was disappointed at first but knew the Lord had something better in mind for me so I waited on Him. The townhouse I looked at had been sold to a man who was transferred to Japan and never moved into it. Within 24 hours, it came back on the market and I bought it! When I first walked into this townhouse I knew, I was home!

I prayed before I started looking for a home of my own and asked the Lord for specific things I would like. I received many more blessings than I could have ever imagined or hoped for. The Lord gave me His very best; an end two-story townhouse with large open rooms, all new white appliances, high ceilings, and more land with woods for privacy overlooking a pond with ducks and geese.

I still to this day am in awe of the blessings of God over my life! I appreciate my townhouse and pray over it every day. I do not take for granted for one moment what God has given me because He gave His very best.

Birthday Surprise

A long time friend and I went to Atlantic Beach to celebrate my birthday! I love the ocean and was looking forward to spending time with her. I had been praying to find a whole sand dollar. Over the years, I had looked for a complete sand dollar but never found one.

Sunday morning we decided to take a walk along the beach and among the broken shells; I saw my whole sand dollar 1-1/2 inches by 1-1/2 inches- perfect, like it had been placed on the beach for me to find it.

I was so excited! I told everyone I met, I found a whole sand dollar and God gave it to me for my birthday!

My friend told me later that she had been coming to Atlantic Beach for 17 years and had never seen a sand dollar much less found a whole one – she said, "me of little faith".

Jeanie prayed and believed God for a complete sand dollar and God gave it to her for her birthday!

Finding Money

A few years ago the Lord gave me an idea to start a tradition on January 1st through December 31st Each coin the Lord placed in my path to pick it up, keep a record and at the end of the year to give all the money I find in an offering to the church to help someone in need.

On each coin is inscribed, "In God We Trust". The Lord showed me to Trust in Him and He will provide the blessings I need in my life.

When a coin is face up, I am looking up to God for my blessings and when a coin is face down, God is looking down to bless me. Either way it is a Blessing from God. I put my money in a large glass cookie jar so I can see my Blessings from God every day.

The first year I gave $22.24 (2,224 blessings from God). Maud and Ron prayed and asked the Lord to multiply the money and the second year I found $84.30 (8,430 blessings from God).

The third year was the most so far, $113.31 (11,331 blessings from God) all in change. Even though I give all the money back to God, I still receive his blessings.

One year, I found a 5-dollar bill and a 1-dollar bill and gave it back to the Lord through an offering. The next year, I found a $1.00 and when I picked it up there was a $5.00 tucked inside. The Lord is so funny!

True happiness comes from giving to someone in need. I always receive more than what I give. It is God's money anyway. My part is to trust Him and He will provide everything I need.

It has been a joy going out each day and wondering what will the Lord bless me with today?

Christmas

Each Christmas, I have bought a live Christmas tree for my townhouse. I pray and ask the Lord for a good price, great shape, and straight top for my porcelain angel, 5 feet in height, and to be delivered. I started a tradition where I buy a hand-painted angel ornament that is dated as a keepsake for each year I have lived in my townhouse.

In December 2001, I went looking for my first Christmas tree in my new townhouse. I was excited and did not know where to look but I prayed that the Lord would help me. I talked to some friends and they said most of the live trees in this area were around $70. I asked the Lord for a Christmas tree around $25 to $40. I went to two different places that sold Christmas trees but the prices were too high and they did not deliver. As I was heading home, I kept praying and then I spotted a large farm that had lots of trees for sale. I pulled in and noticed an older couple sitting by a shed and they said, howdy – I thought I was in the movie, "City Slickers". I liked them right away and knew this was the place I would find my Christmas tree. I found my tree for $25 and a man not only delivered it but set it up for me, too!

My prayers were answered far beyond what I asked for – God gave me my first Christmas tree and it was perfect!

I went back to the large farm, Christmas 2002, where I had bought my first tree but they had raised their prices. As I headed home, I noticed a sign "Christmas Trees for Sale" on a dirt road adjacent to my subdivision. The lady was so nice as I introduced myself and asked if she delivered? She asked me where do you live? I told her I lived in the townhouses and I could carry it to my house. She told me, it is too heavy and you can borrow my jeep and handed me her keys. I paid $20 for the tree and $10 for my wreath! Every time I pray the Lord blesses me with more than I ever ask for or need.

In December 2002, I was talking to a friend on the telephone when I was saying "When the Prayers Go Up, The Blessings Come Down" and the Christmas lights on the top of my tree blinked and I do not have blinking lights. Where the lights blinked are mostly angel ornaments. I got chills after I told her this!

The Christmas of 2003, the lady in my subdivision decided not to sell trees, so I decided to go back to the large farm where I purchased my first Christmas tree. I asked one of the men if he could deliver my tree. I had brought my stand and he put my tree in the stand and loaded it on his pickup. He brought my Christmas tree to my townhouse and set it up in my living room. How's that for service with a smile! Each year has been special blessings from God and it gets better every year.

The Christmas of 2004 was one of the most precious so far! I went back to the large farm where I bought most of my Christmas trees.

At first, when I got to their farm, I did not see anyone around until a woman came out of the house and told me that her husband would be right back.

I had already spotted a Christmas tree lying in a ditch adjacent to the shed and knew immediately that the Lord had already picked this one out for me.

The tag on the tree was $35. When her husband returned, I asked him to hang the tree in the shed so I could see its shape. I had already noticed it had a straight top for my angel ornament. As he was spinning the tree around, he mentioned that he remembered me and that I had bought other trees from him in the past. I told him yes and I would like this tree and could he deliver it? By that time, more people were wandering around and asking questions so I knew it would be some time before I would have my tree delivered. Then he said, I will lower the price to $25 and will deliver it later today.

I decided to see if the tree would fit in my trunk and it did. When I got to my townhouse, the tree needed to be adjusted in the stand before I could bring it inside. It took me a while but I finally got it straight in the stand and placed it in my great room.

When I finished putting on the lights I sat down to admire my tree before starting with the ornaments.

Then the Lord said, go look inside your Christmas tree. I immediately walked to my tree and looked inside the branches and closely nestled to the left side of the trunk was a real baby's bird nest. One of my friends told me when you find a real bird nest in your tree it is God's blessing for your home.

I couldn't believe that the nest didn't come out of the tree; as it was lying in the ditch, transporting it in my trunk, and upside down as I was trying to get it in the stand. God was protecting this baby bird nest!

When I was putting away my Christmas ornaments and taking down my tree, I knew I was going to keep my baby bird nest. I was very careful as I slipped my hand in between the branches and the nest came right out into my hand.

The Lord gave me something extra special this Christmas when He gave me this baby bird nest so I would always have His blessings over my home!

VII. GOD'S PROTECTION

God Cares About You

Have you ever wondered how does God see you? Is he pleased with you or disappointed?

Maybe you feel God has forgotten you, that no one could possibly understand what you are going through, not even God?

Your life matters to God. He cares about you and everything you are going through.

God sees beyond what you are today and what you could be if you trusted Him. He sees your struggles, your broken heart, your lack of faith but He still loves you.

Jesus Christ shed his blood on the cross that God would see us all through his compassion, love and forgiveness.

My prayer is when God sees you; he smiles and says, I am proud of my child!

God's Warning

Each morning after eating breakfast I select a scripture from my scripture box and apply it to my day. The verse I selected was about "trouble" I immediately put it back in my scripture box and selected another verse saying, I do not need any trouble today. I need a verse of encouragement and hope.

Well, my second verse was also about "trouble". I did not realize the Lord was giving me these scriptures on "trouble" to warn me there is a demonic attack ahead and to be in prayer.

When I returned from church, I was eating my lunch and noticed my glass globe on my ceiling fan looked loose. My sofa and glass coffee table are directly below my ceiling fan. As I was standing on my sofa looking up to adjust the globe light, it fell. I immediately yelled out "Jesus" as the globe came crashing down on my glass coffee table. I know the Lord heard my cry for help and protected me from the falling glass.

I just had toe surgery for removal of a sliver of glass 11 days ago and here I am standing barefooted on my sofa and everywhere I looked was glass.

I started thanking the Lord He protected my eyes from the falling glass, the glass on my coffee table was not broken and my baby bird nest, butterfly and other miracles and blessings from the Lord were spared, too!

This scripture says it all, "My help cometh from the Lord who made Heaven and Earth.". Thank You Jesus, for warning me through your scriptures that by calling out your name, you heard my cry for help and rescued me and I am so grateful you did.

God's Peace

      A woman in a black Ford F-150 truck was backing out of a parking space and hit the right side of my car. There was a dent on my right door and she immediately called the police to come. I reassured her that we both were fine and my car could be repaired.

      As we waited together I shared with her that I pray over my car every day for God's protection and He would take care of us. You would have thought, I would be upset over my first dent, but I felt God's peace all around and through me.

      As I continued to pray, the wind started to pick up and there were dark clouds overhead but I still felt God's peace and then a Miracle happened.

      I saw a folded piece of paper blowing towards my feet and it was a $1.00 bill (100 blessings from God). On each bill is written "In God We Trust".

      I shared with her that God sent this $1.00 bill to reassure me that everything would turn out fine. My car was repaired and looks like new and I thank God for His protection and blessings that night! I have learned to pray about everything and it is one of the most important lessons I have learned.

      Philippians 4:6-7 "Don't worry about anything; instead pray about everything tell God your needs and don't forget to thank Him for his answers. If you do this you will experience God's peace, which is far more wonderful than the human mind can understand. His peace will keep your thoughts and your hearts quiet and at rest as you trust in Christ Jesus"…The Living Bible - paraphrased.

God's Timing

As I was sitting in my car with plans to go to the Post Office, I saw a piece of paper in my yard and was debating whether I should take the time to pick it up before I left. Since it had been raining, I would have to go back inside my house, change my shoes and then go around to the back of my house and put it in the trash can. I made the decision to go pick up this paper and throw it away.

As I was approaching the Post Office, I saw two police cars parked on the right side of the road and I looked to the left and saw a car backed up in the woods. I went inside the Post Office and as I was waiting in line a young black woman was telling her story of what happened. Lauren proceeded to tell us that a man was tailgating her on the way to the Post Office and she turned in and parked in a parking space. Lauren was upset about the man following her and was not thinking clearly and left her keys in the ignition with the car still running. As she got out of the car her sweater got caught in the door and she hit reverse. As the car started backwards Lauren was clinging to the car door as her knees were dragged on the pavement. The car headed down a high embankment and across a busy highway where an oncoming car noticed her and started blowing his horn to alert other drivers. The car finally stopped in the woods across from the Post Office.

When the police officers arrived on the scene, they told Lauren that if she had let go of the door the car tires would have rolled over her and she would be dead. Everyone in the Post Office was amazed and saying she was lucky – even the mail lady that waited on me said the same thing. I told her luck had nothing to do with it God was protecting her, her guardian angels were watching over her.

I asked Lauren if her life flashed before her and she said, no. As Lauren set with her bloody knees exposed she told me they hurt and I told her God spared your life today and I will be praying for you.

As I drove out of the Post Office I saw the tire tracks where Lauren's car had traveled down the embankment and where it ended up. I was amazed over her story and what had just happened and then the Holy Spirit revealed to me about my delay getting to the Post Office. If I had left earlier I would have been involved in this accident. I would not have seen Lauren's car flying down the embankment to my right. She would have hit me and we both would be dead. I started to cry because I realized that God is always protecting me. Picking up one piece of trash in my yard delayed me from being in an accident.

God spared my life and Lauren's today and I'm so glad He did!

VIII. SIGNS AND WONDERS

Hearing God's Voice

I have been asked does the Lord talk to you and my answer is Yes He does; sometimes He speaks to the Holy Spirit within me, sometimes He talks to me through my Spiritual Dreams, and a few times I have heard an Audible Voice. I am open to however the Lord chooses to communicate with me.

I have been asked how did you know it was the Lord talking to you and not the devil. The Lord talks to me in a way that I will understand Him. The Lord is love and kindness and would never hurt or abuse my trust in Him. He brings forth light not darkness, fear and despair.

I was in a job that was stressful and not the best working environment but I knew the Lord wanted me to stay. As the weeks went by I was being tested to see if I would remain true to the Lord.

I sense my time at this company was coming to an end. As I was walking down the hall a young woman was approaching me; and these were the words spoken to me…"She is here to replace you." It was a man's voice and I was so excited to hear a whole sentence from the Lord!

The Lord answered my prayers and I passed the test. That afternoon I was let go from this company and never looked back. I was free to go with His blessings.

Lord, I'm Here

My radio music came on slowly and as I awoke heard my first name spoken out loud. It was a man's voice and at first I thought the voice was coming from the radio but I heard it correctly.

I was not afraid but no other words were spoken to me.

When the Lord wants to get your full attention, He calls you by name. I answered I'm here, Lord!

Each day is exciting because I do not know how the Lord is going to communicate with me. My part is to listen, pray and be open to His will.

Time is so precious between the Lord and me. The desire of my heart is to stay focused to what He needs for me to do for Him each day.

Word from God

When I awoke this was the only word spoken to me, "Done".

I did not know why I received this word but knew the Lord was preparing my heart for something special.

I bought my first new townhouse with His Blessings.

The Lord was letting me know 3 months ahead of time – everything is in place, "Done"!

Rainbows and Clouds

In 1995, I was riding in a car with two other people when I looked up in the sky and saw a Vertical Rainbow. It was so beautiful and I was moved and excited in my Spirit. It was a sunny day and it had not been raining. Most Rainbows are curved and horizontal across the skyline but this Vertical Rainbow went straight up into the sky like a stairwell to Heaven.

The Vertical Rainbow colors I have seen are red, yellow, and green. The colors have specific meaning: Red means God's Passion, Yellow is God's Gift and Green is God's Love.

When I see a Vertical Rainbow they are to the left or right of the sun and it has not been raining. Curved Rainbows are seen directly across from the sun not beside it.

Every time I see a Vertical Rainbow I feel more connected to the Lord.

On February 22, 2004, three days before the movie, "The Passion of the Christ" opened I saw a beautiful Vertical Rainbow. As I was looking at the Rainbow, God gave me a Vision of an Eternity Circle on top of a Cross through the Rainbow.

The Eternity Circle represented the head of Christ on the Cross. This Vertical Rainbow was facing the movie theatre where the "The Passion of the Christ" was going to be released. It was exactly 7 weeks to Easter Sunday and the number 7 means complete and God's approval on this movie.

In March 2005, I was in my car and looked up into the sky and the Lord gave me a Vision of a large solid white Quill Pen in the shape of a cloud.

The pages of the Bible were written with the Quill Pen and I am honored that the Lord used the Quill Pen as a Vision to show me His signature of approval on this book.

God has shown me wonderful expressions of His love through Vertical Rainbows and Clouds and it is a reminder to me that the Lord will be returning soon and to keep my eyes on the sky

Angel of Light

I was going through a difficult time in my life when I was a little girl. We had moved, my mother had remarried, and I was in a new school.

All of these changes created stress and confusion and I prayed to the Lord for his help! The Lord heard my cries and gave me my first Vision – an Angel of Light.

As I was sleeping, I felt a hand on my left shoulder with a slight pressure that caused me to awake. I opened my eyes and saw the most beautiful white Angel of Light standing next to my bed.

This Angel did not have a face and at first I was frightened. I closed my eyes tight and pinched myself to see if I was awake and I was.

I knew this Angel of Light came to reassure me that I was not alone the Lord was with me.

IX. HEAVEN BOUND

Balanced Life

How do you know if your life is out of balance? Have you lost your sense of humor? Are you stressed out? Do you worry? These are some of the ways to know your life is out of balance.

Living a balanced life starts with keeping your priorities in order:

First key is to pray. It is the most important key in staying balanced in all areas of your life.

Second key is to make time to spend with God. Talk to God and also listen to His voice. His desire is to have a relationship with you.

Third key is to meditate on God's word, the Bible. This is where you will find strength, wisdom and understanding to help you walk in your faith.

Fourth key is to laugh. Laughter keeps your heart happy and your whole life in balanced.

Conviction and Belief

You may have been praying for a long time for family members or friends to come to Christ and all you see is them running away from God. Each person has to make their own decision about whether they will follow Christ.

A few years ago, a pastor wrote a statement for the unsaved and received remarkable results for salvation. Before I say this statement, I hold the Bible, which is the Sword of the Spirit, in my hands.

This statement needs to be spoken out loud with conviction and belief to the devil because he holds your love ones under his control: "In the name of Jesus, you foul devil demon of hell that binds (fill in the person's name) _____'s soul. I bind you in Jesus' name. I claim his/her/their salvation and deliverance in the name of the Lord Jesus Christ" and date it.

Everyday speak this statement out loud and you will see unsaved family and friends come to Christ. You never have to say a word, just show them God's love and the Lord will take care of the rest.

Heaven

How can you be sure you are going to Heaven? In John 14:6 "Jesus said, I am the way, and the truth, and the life, no one comes to the Father but by me."

When I accepted Jesus Christ into my heart, my focus changed from the desires of this world to God's Will for my life. As I prayed and asked for forgiveness of my sins, Jesus answered my prayers.

This is the most important Prayer to pray for Salvation. I am a sinner. I believe Jesus Christ, your Son, died on the cross for my sins and rose from the dead to be my Lord. I repent of my sins and personally invite Jesus Christ into my heart. Thank you, Jesus for giving me your free gift of eternal life.

Please help me live my life for you as you reveal yourself through your word, the Bible, in Jesus' name I pray.

Your name is now written in the Lamb's Book of Life.

Get Ready!

Now that you have accepted Jesus Christ into your heart you are ready to start moving forward into the things of God. All of this does not happen overnight. You are a work in progress. I know from my own experience that if you can learn the lessons you go through the first time, you will not have to repeat them again. But one thing I do know you are not alone, you have someone that is your biggest encourager and friend, Jesus Christ.

Enjoy the journey and learn to appreciate what you have. This makes life so much more enjoyable. Things are not as important as letting God use your life for His higher purpose and plan.

Letting go of control is not always easy but when you are trusting Jesus to help you, your life will blossom and grow far and beyond anything this world has to offer.

Remember this is not dress rehearsal; this is real life that will last into eternity. God speed…

Eternity

We are living in a world that is unsure what is going to happen next. It all comes down to what do you believe? Do you believe that Jesus Christ died for you?

John 3-16 states "For God so loved the world that He gave His only begotten Son, that whosoever believeth in Him should not perish, but have eternal life".

Father God is the only one who knows when His Son, Jesus Christ will return to this earth and take his children home.

Eternity is forever and ever! You will live two places when you die or leave this earth; Heaven with Jesus or Hell with the devil.

Where will you spend Eternity?

Jeanie Jones grew up in Georgia and started writing at a young age. She went to church with her family but did not have a personal relationship with Jesus Christ. Her parents were invited to be witnesses on a Lay Witness Mission in Coffeyville, Kansas and persuaded Jeanie and her brother to go along. She really didn't want to go but decided to make it fun when they told her there would be teenagers and a band.

As Jeanie looked around, she saw young people that had a joy and peace like she'd never seen before. They were happy and she wanted what they had! That Saturday night the sanctuary was dark except where the band was playing on stage. Jeanie says she "felt a gentle urging in her spirit to go forward." From the left side of the altar, she heard someone crying and it was her brother, Bill at the far right end. Jeanie and Bill both accepted Jesus Christ into their hearts at 11:00 p.m. on April 15, 1972.

In August 2002, she became a published poet in Honesty Awakened. Jeanie says, "receiving the Editor's Choice Award for *Love and Trust in Him* was one of the highlights of my life. This was the first poem that the Lord gave me after accepting Jesus into my heart." In March 2005, the Lord inspired Jeanie to write **The Desires of My Heart.** She says, "I prayed and asked the Holy Spirit to help me and he did. We worked so well together that four hours seemed like a minute. It was incredible!

When I completed this book, I still did not have a title but prayed and waited on the Lord. On August 19, 2006, the title and covers were revealed to me through a vision on my great-grandfather's birthday!

I am currently working on The Man in My Dreams, a love story that has taken over 30 years of waiting on God."

www.ingramcontent.com/pod-product-compliance
Lightning Source LLC
Chambersburg PA
CBHW051708040426
42446CB00008B/772